D1198894

RG

GREATEST WARRIORS
VIKINGS

PHILIP STEELE

ARCTURUS

This edition first published in 2014 by Arcturus Publishing

Distributed by Black Rabbit Books
P.O. Box 3263
Mankato
Minnesota MN 56002

Edited and designed by: Discovery Books Ltd.

Library of Congress Cataloging-in-Publication Data

Steele, Philip, 1948-
Vikings / Philip Steele.
    pages cm. -- (Greatest warriors)
  Includes index.
  Summary: "Provides readers with exciting details, facts, and statistics about Vikings"--Provided by publisher.
  Audience: Grades 4-6.
  ISBN 978-1-78212-403-0 (library binding)
 1. Vikings--Juvenile literature. I. Title.
  DL66.S78 2014
  948'.022--dc23

                            2013005688

Series concept: Joe Harris
Managing editor for Discovery Books: Laura Durman
Editor: Clare Collinson
Picture researcher: Clare Collinson
Designer: Ian Winton

The publisher would like to thank Hurstwic re-enactment group (www.hurstwic.org) and the Irish National Heritage Park, Wexford, Ireland, for their help in the preparation of this book.

Picture credits:
Alamy: p. 6 (Christian Hartmann), p. 12t (Ladi Kirn), p. 13t (Adrian Buck), p. 14 (Photos 12), p. 24l inset (Troy GB images); Corbis: p. 5 (Ted Spiegel), p. 8 (Anna Volkova), p. 22 (SALVADOR SAS/epa), p. 28 (Bob Singleton/Demotix); Getty Images: p. 4 (Photoshot); Hurstwic: pp. 12b, 13b; iStockphoto.com: p. 29b (AndrewJShearer); Shutterstock Images: pp. title, 16 (Arne Bramsen), p. 7 background (Gabriela Insuratelu), p. 9r (Bodil1955), p. 10 (Microprisma), pp. 11, 21 (tovovan), p. 15 (OlegDoroshin), p. 24r (Ron Zmiri); Wikimedia Commons: pp. 7 front, 29t (Wolfgang Sauber), p. 9l (Johnbod), p. 17 (Portable Antiquities Scheme), pp. 18, 20, 27 (Jagro), p. 19 (Magnus Manske), p. 23 (Nachosan), p. 25 (Trollhead), p. 26 (Butko).
Cover images: Shutterstock Images: top (tovovan), bottom centre (i4lcocl2), background (Gabriela Insuratelu).

Printed in China

SL002669US
Supplier 03, Date 0513, Print Run 2360

CONTENTS

VIKING RAIDERS!

From the eighth to the eleventh centuries CE, fierce seaborne **raiders** struck fear in communities throughout Europe. They sailed from the lands we call Scandinavia—Denmark, Sweden, and Norway. They wanted **plunder**, power, trade, and land. The strangers were usually known as Vikings, or sometimes Northmen or Danes.

SHOCK ATTACK

During an attack, Viking warriors stormed ashore to rob churches and villages. They killed many people and left buildings in flames.

THE FEAR SPREADS

The Viking terror raged across Europe, from Britain and Ireland to Germany and France. The Vikings sailed southward, too, and settled in Russia to the east. They even crossed the North Atlantic.

BLOODAXE AND IRONSIDE

The first Vikings fought in the name of Odin, their mighty god of war. We can still read about Viking adventures in old stories called sagas. The names of the greatest Viking warriors and kings are still remembered today—Björn Ironside, Eirik Bloodaxe, Ivar the Boneless, and Sigurd Snake-in-the-Eye.

SEABORNE RAIDERS

The Vikings went to war in **longships**. The sight of their sails on the horizon created panic among communities on shore. By the ninth century, Viking ships were prowling the seas in great numbers.

BATTLE REPORT

Raid on Lindisfarne, 793

On June 8, 793, Vikings attacked a monastery on the island of Lindisfarne, off the northeast coast of England. Many of the Christian monks who lived in the monastery were killed. The Vikings carried off treasure and burned down the church. The attack was not the first Viking raid, but it was so brutal that it shocked all of Europe.

BATTLE READY

Most Viking men spent much of their time farming or fishing. However, they were also warriors—skilled in the use of spears, axes, and swords—who were ready for battle at any time. Sometimes they fought each other in family quarrels called feuds. When called upon, they sailed off to foreign lands in search of riches.

OFF ON A RAID
In the spring or fall, many Vikings left their villages to go raiding, led by their local chieftain, or **jarl**.

NEW LANDS
Sometimes raiders stayed abroad over the winter. They set up camps to keep control of land they had won. Later, Vikings began to settle and make permanent new homes in these lands.

CALL TO ARMS

In later Viking times, there were powerful kings, but they did not have full-time armies. When they needed troops, they sent a messenger to the local jarl. The jarl had just five days to raise a ship's crew of warriors to fight for the king.

THE JARL

The jarl was the most important man in the Viking community. He called up warriors to go raiding or to fight in battles.

FIGHTING TALK

Training

Viking boys learned how to handle a boat, how to wrestle, and how to use axes or knives. Older boys were taught to fight with swords and spears. By the age of 16, they were anxious to leave home and go raiding.

WEAPONS OF WAR

Weapons such as swords and axes were the most precious possessions that many Viking families owned. The best weapons were handed down from father to son. They were often given nicknames such as "Sword-breaker," "Odin's Flame," or "Leg-biter."

SPEAR

One of the most useful Viking weapons was the spear. It was used for both thrusting and throwing. The iron spearhead was joined to a shaft made of wood from ash trees.

IRON SWORD

Viking swords were made of iron. The blades were grooved and double-edged in steel. They were used with a slashing action.

BATTLE-AX

The battle-ax had a curved iron blade wedged onto a wooden **haft**.

DEATH AT A DISTANCE

Swords, spears, and axes were the most useful weapons in hand-to-hand combat. For long-distance attacks, Vikings used bows and arrows made of wood from yew, elm, or ash trees. Arrows were fitted with arrowheads made of iron.

SWORD SPLENDOR

This richly decorated sword **hilt** would have been very costly to make— a sign that its owner was wealthy and had high status.

ARROW ATTACK

Bows and arrows were often used at the start of battles to attack the enemy before close combat began.

COMBAT STATS

Weapons data

- **Length of sword blade:** 28-32 inches (70-80 cm)
- **Length of spear:** shaft 6.5-10 feet (2-3 m); spearhead up to 20 inches (50 cm)
- **Length of bow:** 75 inches (190 cm); minimum range about 273 yards (250 m)
- **Length of arrow:** shaft about 28 inches (70 cm); arrowhead about 4-6 inches (10-15 cm)
- **Small battle-ax:** total weight 28 ounces (800 g)

BATTLE ARMOR

The good thing about armor was that it protected the body during battle. The bad thing was that it was heavy, and it cost a lot, too. Viking raiders needed to be quick on their feet. Generally, they wore little armor, either by choice or necessity.

FIGHTING LIGHT
Most Viking warriors fought in everyday attire. They wore a cap, a woolen tunic, pants, and leather shoes.

SHIRT OF MAIL
Top fighters might wear a **byrnie**, an outer shirt of **chain mail**. It was made up of small iron rings. Each ring was linked to the four ones next to it.

THE ROUND SHIELD

To protect their bodies, Vikings tended to rely on their shields rather than body armor. Shields were round and often painted with bright patterns. They were made of wood. The planks were sometimes covered in leather, making it more difficult for the shield to split. The rim was bound with leather, too. An iron **boss** in the center protected the hand.

IRON HELMET

Most iron helmets were conical or round, with bars to protect the nose. The finest helmets had a full guard to protect the cheeks and eyes.

COMBAT STATS

Shield data

- **Diameter:** about 39 inches (1 m)
- **Weight:** about 11-15 pounds (5-7 kg)
- **Boss:** about 6 inches (15 cm) in diameter

The Vikings went to battle in ships and on horseback, but they generally fought on foot. The key to their success was violent one-to-one combat. As their weapons clashed, the warriors shoved, kicked, jumped, and dived.

SPEAR ATTACK

In close combat, an attacker would thrust the tip of his spear at his opponent, while the defender tried to stop the attack with his shield.

SHIELD SLAM

A Viking's shield not only provided protection. It served as a weapon, used for slamming, shoving, and hitting.

IN FOR THE KILL

Viking combat was brutal and deadly. A fighter targeted the least protected parts of his opponent's body. A cut to the legs could stop him in his tracks, and attacks on the head and neck were often fatal.

AX ON AX

An ax blade could smash through a helmet or destroy a shield. It could also be used to hook an arm or leg, or a shield rim. The back end could deliver a knockout blow.

FIGHTING TALK

Trial by combat

Under Viking law, a dispute between two people could be settled by combat instead of by a trial. The fight had to take place in front of a public **assembly**. The rules varied, as did the weapons. Combat often ended when the first blood was drawn.

SAILING TO WAR

The Vikings were skilled sailors. Longships were used for major voyages, as well as for raiding and warfare. A longship was narrow, streamlined, and light enough to skim over the waves. It was shallow enough to sail along rivers or haul up a beach.

MAST
A longship's mast supported a large sail made of wool or linen.

CUTTHROAT CREW
On board was a crew of 30 or more, each one of them a warrior as well as an oarsman. They sat on chests as they rowed, not on benches.

HULL
The overlapping planks of the **hull** were made waterproof with wool and **resin**.

BATTLES AT SEA

Vikings mostly attacked their enemies along coasts or rivers. Sea battles were less common. When they did take place, ships might be lashed together and used as fighting platforms. The fighting took place hand-to-hand, just as it did on land.

DRAGON PROW

Viking longships often had carved **prows** decorated with a snarling dragon's head. The **figurehead** was designed to scare off evil spirits—and the enemy!

COMBAT STATS

Longship data

- **Length:** about 75 feet (23 m)
- **Mast height:** about 52 feet (16 m)
- **Sail width:** about 40 feet (12 m)
- **Average speed:** 5-10 knots (6-11 mph or 9-18 km/h)
- **Top speed:** 15 knots (17 mph or 28 km/h)

RAIDS AND PLUNDER

Viking raiders tried to take the enemy by surprise. They might row up a river by night or under the cover of mist. They would suddenly appear as if from nowhere. With their dragon ships, swords, and axes, they were a terrifying sight.

WARFARE ON THE RUN
Raiders moved at top speed, launching rapid attacks. Larger armies needed to occupy and control the land, but raiders wanted to seize their plunder and get away quickly.

PLUNDER AND DEVASTATION

Vikings carried off gold and silver coins, jewelry, crosses, and bells. Churches were easy targets because monks and priests were not fighters. The raiders might also steal crops or animals. Sometimes they kidnapped people and sold them into slavery. Viking raiders often set fire to the villages they attacked, spreading panic far and wide.

PRECIOUS HOARD

These coins and bracelets are part of a tenth-century Viking **hoard** discovered in Silverdale, Lancashire, in September 2011. Containing over 200 pieces, it is one of the largest Viking hoards ever discovered in the UK.

BATTLE REPORT

The Iona raids

A monastery was founded on the island of Iona, in Scotland, in the sixth century. The monastery became an important holy place for Christian **pilgrims**, who brought gold and silver as gifts. To the Vikings, Iona was the perfect target. From 794, they made a series of raids, plundering the monastery's treasure and killing many of the monks. In the ninth century, the remaining treasures were moved to Ireland and mainland Scotland for safekeeping, and eventually, the monastery was abandoned.

GRAND ARMIES

From the 860s, Viking chieftains and rulers began to form alliances and raise large armies. They attacked big towns and even cities such as Hamburg, London, and Paris. These warriors were not raiders—they were invaders!

INVASION FORCE
Large armies of Viking warriors were assembled to attack England in the 860s and 870s.

DANES IN ENGLAND

Viking armies conquered a large area of England known as the **Danelaw**. They founded a kingdom that covered much of northern England, with a capital at Yorvik (modern York). It was many years before they were defeated.

PAYOFF TIME

The Vikings soon found that weak rulers would pay them just to go away. In the 800s and 900s, both **Frankish** and **Anglo-Saxon** kings paid out a fortune. But the Vikings always came back for more.

LAND GRABBER

Meet the Viking leader named Rollo. In 911, the Franks gave him the ultimate payoff—a whole region of their country. It became known as the "land of the Northmen," or Normandy. In return, Rollo agreed to protect the Franks from further Viking invasions.

ROLLON

BATTLE REPORT

Siege of Paris, 885

Attacking cities required a different kind of fighting—**siege warfare**. In November 885, a large army of Vikings sailed up the Seine River in France. They surrounded Paris and attacked the city's walls with giant **catapults** and **battering rams** for nearly a year. Many defenders died, but the city was not captured.

PITCHED BATTLE

In the 800s and 900s, Viking warriors took part in many fierce battles. They could not win new lands, where they could settle and trade, without a bloody fight. Each battle would open with a single spear thrown at the enemy—in honor of the god Odin.

THE CHARGE

After the first spear had been thrown, showers of arrows and spears were aimed at the enemy. Then the king led a charge. If he was threatened, his personal guards closed ranks around him, shield to shield. They formed a shield wall.

SHIELD WALL
A shield wall could only be broken by brute force and sheer weight of numbers.

THE HOUSECARLS

Members of the royal bodyguard were called "housecarls." They were loyal **elite** troops who had a special duty to protect the king in battle and fight with him to the bitter end.

FREE-FOR-ALL
As the ranks broke up, sword blows and thrusting spears clashed, and the hand-to-hand fighting became desperate.

BATTLE REPORT

Battle of Stamford Bridge, 1066

The Battle of Stamford Bridge was one of the last great battles of the Viking age. It was fought in Yorkshire, England, on September 25, 1066. On one side was the Anglo-Saxon king, Harold Godwinson, commanding 15,000 troops. On the other was Tostig Godwinson, Harold's brother, in alliance with a famous Viking invader, King Harald Hardrada of Norway. Hardrada had 300 ships and 9,000 troops. The English defeated the invaders, and Hardrada and Tostig were killed along with 6,000 of their warriors.

BERSERK!

We use the word *berserk* in modern English to describe a person whose behavior is wild and out of control. In Viking times, berserkers were a group of warriors who were famous for their fury in battle. It was said they would wrestle with boulders in their frenzy!

BATTLE RAGE

Before battle, berserkers worked themselves into an almost uncontrollable rage. When fighting, they showed fantastic strength and complete lack of fear. In the thirteenth century, the Icelandic poet Snorri Sturluson said berserkers were as strong as bulls and that they bit their shields in fury.

BEARSKIN
It is possible that the word "berserker" comes from a word meaning "wearer of the bear shirt." If so, it may describe a bearskin worn in battle.

ODIN'S OWN

Some berserkers may have believed that the god Odin gave them special superhuman powers. Like all Vikings, they believed that brave warriors who were killed in battle would dine in the great hall of the gods, which they called "Valhalla."

SHOCK TROOPS

Harald Fairhair, who ruled Norway from 872 to 930, used berserkers as elite **shock troops**. Other Viking kings used them as bodyguards.

THE CRUNCHER

This is a Viking chess piece, carved from the tusk of a walrus. It shows a berserker in such a rage that he is chewing the edge of his shield.

FIGHTING TALK

Shapeshifters

Some people believed that in battle, a berserker could change his form into that of a wolf. In a poem composed around 900, the Norwegian poet Hornklofi also links berserkers with wolves: "Wolf-coats are they called, those who bear swords stained with blood in the battle." The connection between berserkers and wolves may have contributed to the development of the werewolf myth in Europe.

WARRIORS ON THE DEFENSE

Even when they were not on raids, Viking warriors were always at risk of being attacked. To defend themselves against their enemies, they surrounded their camps, towns, and villages with watchtowers, ditches, and fences.

HOME DEFENDER
Viking warriors were at their fiercest when defending their own homes.

WARRIOR'S LONGHOUSE
Viking warriors lived with their families in rectangular houses called longhouses. The houses had sloping roofs covered in turf or thatch. Inside, they usually had one long room, which was sometimes divided up into smaller rooms.

EARTHWORK DEFENSES

Viking warriors built defenses from timber, earth, and stone. Their longest **earthwork** was the Danevirke, in Jutland, Denmark. Begun in 737, it was about 18 miles (30 km) long and up to 20 feet (6 m) high.

MILITARY BASES

The ultimate Viking fortresses were circular **ring forts**, built in Denmark and Sweden in the 900s, when Harald Bluetooth was king of Denmark. The forts were used as **garrisons** for troops.

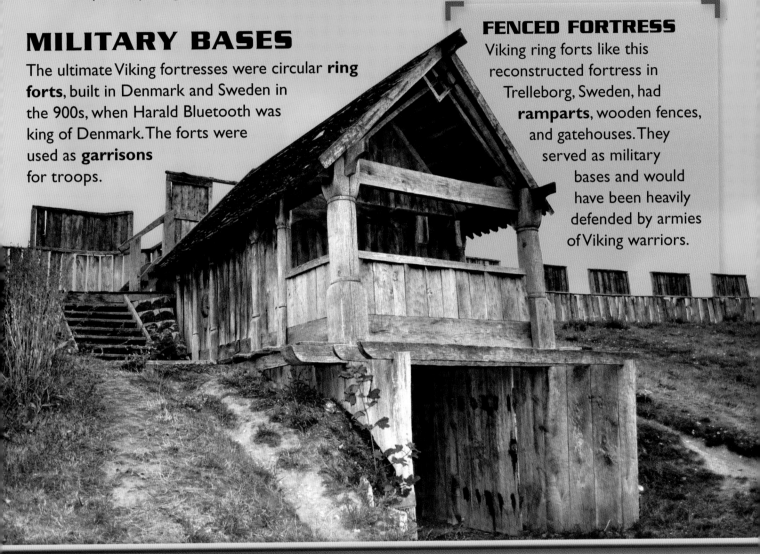

FENCED FORTRESS

Viking ring forts like this reconstructed fortress in Trelleborg, Sweden, had **ramparts**, wooden fences, and gatehouses. They served as military bases and would have been heavily defended by armies of Viking warriors.

FIGHTING TALK

Jomsborg

The part-legendary Jomsvikings were said to be a band of elite Viking warriors living in the 900s and 1000s. Their famous ring fort was called the Jomsborg. It was built on an island, perhaps Wolin in the Baltic Sea off the coast of Poland. Its harbor was defended by a stone tower with catapults—and it could be sealed off with a gate of iron.

WARRIORS OF THE WORLD

The ninth and tenth centuries were a time of great expansion for the Vikings. They settled in Iceland and Greenland. They fought with the native warriors of North America and crossed the snows of Russia. Some of the most famous Vikings of all were based in Turkey.

VIKING SETTLERS

In the ninth century, Vikings known as Varangians settled in parts of modern-day Russia. The Varangian chieftain, Rurik, founded a powerful **dynasty** that ruled Russia until the seventeenth century.

WARRIORS' WELCOME
Here, the Varangian chieftain Rurik and his brothers Sineus and Truvor are being welcomed by the people of Ladoga, Russia. They invited Rurik to protect and rule over them.

ELITE RECRUITS

In the 900s, Varangian Vikings were hired to serve the **Byzantine Empire**, whose capital they called Miklagard (now Istanbul in Turkey). In 988, the Byzantine emperor, Basil II, decided to form a personal bodyguard made up of elite Vikings. It was called the Varangian Guard.

VARANGIAN GUARDSMAN

The Varangian Guard were heavily armored warriors who protected the Byzantine emperor from his many enemies. They also fought in wars. They were reserved for the trickiest point in any battle.

FIGHTING TALK

The great escape

The Golden Horn, a sea inlet at Istanbul, was sealed off from the open sea by chains stretched across the entrance. Having been thrown in prison, Harald Hardrada, a former commander of the Varangian Guard, set about making an escape. Upon reaching the chains, he and his men rocked their longship backward and forward so that it "seesawed" over the harbor chains.

VIKING TWILIGHT

By the eleventh century, times were changing. The kingdoms of Europe were becoming better defended against raids and invasions. Longship crews could no longer sail where they pleased and take what they wanted. The Viking age was coming to an end.

THE NEW WARFARE

Toward the end of the 1000s, **cavalry** was being used more on the battlefield. The shield was now long and kite-shaped, offering better protection on horseback.

FIGHTING TALK

The coming of the knights

The mounted horseman clad in chain mail soon became the most important type of soldier. In Europe and Western Asia, the next 400 years would belong to the knight in armor and the builders of castles.

VIKING PRIEST

The Christian faith came to the Viking lands in the 900s and 1000s. Raiding warriors could no longer kill monks in the name of the god Odin.

THE NORMANS

The old spirit of the Vikings lived on in Normandy. The Normans spoke French, but—like their Viking ancestors—they were furious and ruthless fighters. They invaded large areas of Europe. They built "motte-and-bailey" castles—high mounds topped by wooden and later stone towers.

A FIERY FAREWELL

The story of the Vikings still fascinates people today. At the Up Helly Aa festival in Shetland, Scotland, a replica longship is set ablaze. It is easy to imagine that a dead Viking chieftain is being welcomed to Valhalla, the great hall of the gods.

GLOSSARY

Anglo-Saxon referring to the people whose kings ruled in England at the time of the Vikings

assembly a public gathering. Viking assemblies made laws and passed judgement

battering ram a length of heavy timber used to break down gates and walls

berserker a Viking warrior who worked himself up into a rage before battle

boss the central knob on a shield

byrnie a shirt or tunic made of chain mail

Byzantine Empire an empire in Southeast Europe, Asia Minor, and North Africa, formed from the eastern part of the Roman Empire

catapult a machine designed to hurl stones or other missiles at the enemy

cavalry troops on horseback

chain mail a type of armor made of interlinking iron rings

Danelaw the parts of England occupied by Danish Vikings

dynasty a succession of related rulers

earthwork mounds of soil raised as a defensive barrier or wall

elite describing a small group of people considered the best

figurehead a carving that decorates the front of a ship

Frankish describing the people whose kings ruled in France at the time of the Vikings

garrison a base for armed troops

haft the handle of an ax or other weapon

hilt the handle of a sword

hoard a store of valued objects that has been hidden away

hull the body of a ship

jarl a Viking chieftain, earl, or prince

longship a long, fast ship used by the Vikings

pilgrim a person who travels to a certain place for religious reasons

plunder stolen goods

prow the front end of a ship

raider someone who attacks a place and carries off stolen goods

ramparts raised defenses of stone or earth

resin sticky sap from a pine tree

ring fort any large, round earthwork built by Vikings

shock troops troops specially chosen to lead an attack

siege warfare surrounding a town or castle and cutting off its supplies

FURTHER INFORMATION

Books

Anglo-Saxon and Viking Britain by Alex Woolf (Franklin Watts, 2012)

The Anglo-Saxons and Vikings by Hazel Maskell and Abigail Wheatley (Usborne, 2012)

Viking (Eyewitness) by Dorling Kindersley (Dorling Kindersley, 2011)

Vikings (Children in History) by Katie Jackson Bedford (Franklin Watts, 2011)

Vikings (Warriors: Age of Conquerors) by Philip Wilkinson (Carlton Books, 2008)

The Vikings in Britain by Moira Butterfield (Franklin Watts, 2013)

Web Sites

Viking Age History

www.hurstwic.org/history/text/history.htm

A site packed with awesome features, videos, photos, and links that cover all aspects of life in the Viking Age, including Viking arms, armor, combat training, ships, raids, longhouses, society, and religion.

Viking Longship

www.smithsonianmag.com/history-archaeology/Raiders-or-Traders. html

Explore the *Sea Stallion*, a replica Viking vessel built to help archaeologists discover how and why the Vikings set off for distant lands. This fascinating feature from the Smithsonian web site includes a video about the replica's construction and sea voyage from Roskilde, Denmark, to Dublin, Ireland.

The Vikings

www.pbs.org/wgbh/nova/vikings/

Discover this amazing introduction to the Viking world on the PBS/Nova web site. Packed with videos, photos, and features that explore the secrets of Norse ships, secrets of the Viking sword, a reconstructed Viking village, detailed maps, the rune system of writing, and much more.

Index

Anglo-Saxons 19, 21
armies 7, 16, 18–19, 21, 25
armor 10–11, 27, 28
axes 6, 7, 8, 9, 13, 16

battles 6, 7, 9, 20–21, 27, 28
  berserkers 22, 23
  one-to-one 12, 13, 15
  sea 15
  sieges 19
berserkers 22–23
Bluetooth, Harald 25
bows and arrows 9, 20
Britain 4

chain mail 10, 28
chieftains 6, 18, 26, 29
Christians 17, 29
churches 4, 5, 17

Danelaw 18
Danevirke 25
Denmark 4, 25

earthworks 25
England 5, 18, 21

Fairhair, Harald 23
fires 4, 5, 17, 29
forts 25
France 4, 19, 29

garrisons 25
Germany 4
Godwinson, Harold 21
Godwinson, Tostig 21

Hardrada, Harald 21, 27
helmets 11, 13
housecarls 21

invasions 18, 19, 21, 28
Iona 17
Ireland 4, 17
Istanbul 27

jarls 6, 7
Jomsvikings 25

kings 5, 7, 19, 21, 25
  bodyguards 20, 21, 23, 27
knights 28

Lindisfarne 5
longhouses 24
longships 5, 14–15, 16, 21, 27, 28, 29

Miklagard 27
monasteries 5, 17

Normans 19, 29
Norway 4, 21, 23, 24

Odin 5, 20, 23, 29

Paris, Siege of 19

raids 4, 6, 7, 16–17, 24, 28, 29
  Iona 17
  Lindisfarne 5
ring forts 25
Rollo 19
Rurik 26
Russia 4, 26

sagas 5
Scotland 17, 29
shields 11, 12, 13, 20, 28
  berserkers 22, 23
sieges 19
Silverdale hoard 17
spears 6, 7, 8, 9, 12, 20, 21
Stamford Bridge, Battle of 21
Sweden 4, 25
swords 6, 7, 8, 9, 16, 21

training 7

Valhalla 23, 29
Varangians 26, 27
villages 4, 6, 17, 24

weapons 6, 7, 8–9, 12, 13, 16, 19, 20, 21, 25

Yorvik 18